ZULU
TRIBAL HERITAGE

• ZULU TRIBAL HERITAGE •

SOUND OF DRUMS

From early childhood, Zulus, like other people of Africa, love to sing and dance. Social gatherings inevitably involve dancing, no matter what time of day or night. Zulu dancers are happy to exhibit their skills – and their fitness – without a trace of inhibition. While dance routines are often highly structured, they also reflect strong elements of improvisation as a performer responds to his or her mood of the moment. Ceremonial dances are spectacular to watch, whether they involve large crowds gyrating, clapping and stamping their feet, or small groups taking turns at showing off their individual talents

• TRADITIONAL DANCING •

to the accompaniment and encouragement of drum rhythms, singing, whistling and ululating. Zulu dancing embodies the traditions and lore of the various clans, with men and boys usually performing separately from their womenfolk. The dances of men, for instance, might reflect stylized battle movements or describe the whipped-up energy which generates courage before a hunting expedition, as opposed to some humorous story-telling element in a women's dance. Dancing also occurs casually outside a hut or along a roadside, and often embodies an element of social commentary about some ordinary event of everyday life.

• ZULU TRIBAL HERITAGE •

CLASH OF ARMS

The celebration of military might and physical courage are constant threads which run through the fabric of Zulu culture. As part of its Shakan legacy, these are central to the oral tradition and ceremonies which keep Zulu history alive, and embody the great deeds and accomplishments of the famous regiments or *Amabutho*. From an early age, young boys learn the intricacies of stick fighting. This competitive form

• STICK FIGHTING •

of martial art is practised with great skill, discipline and relish by both young and mature Zulu males, either as teams or as individual contestants. The fighters carry a small shield made of ox hide in the left hand, while the right holds a stick approximately a metre long. This is used to strike principally at the opponent's head although injuries inflicted elsewhere on the body are not discounted. Strength and agility play important roles in achieving success in this often dangerous sport which is usually conducted in a spirit of good humour, although tempers can become frayed. As adolescents in traditional Zulu communities, boys enter youth regiments to be trained for the rigours of manhood.

• ZULU TRIBAL HERITAGE •

SHIELDS AND SPEARS

Weapons were and still are an integral part of the Zulu tradition and men carry variously sized wooden staffs and clubs as part of their attire. In pre-Shakan times tribes used throwing spears or assegais to fight each other for cattle or grazing rights. Shaka introduced the famous short stabbing spear to enforce fighting at close combat. This deadly weapon proved so devastating to opponents that it was still in use sixty years later during the Anglo-Zulu wars. But pitted against the heavy artillery of the British, its shortcomings became obvious. To a large extent it replaced the longer assegai which was hurled at the enemy from a distance. Shaka ridiculed the logic of a striking

TRADITIONAL WEAPONS

force which rendered itself defenceless by throwing its weapons away. Zulu blacksmiths used primitive foundries to forge their spearheads and these are still found in remote rural areas, although this skill has become increasingly rare. Body-length shields were designed both as a protective device and to conceal the weapons an *impi* or warrior was carrying. The small ceremonial shield used in stick fighting is also carried while dancing. Zulu shields are made of oxhide stretched on the ground and secured with pegs before being cut to the required shape. Decorative slits are cut in the centre of the hide with a strong staff threaded through them as a handle, which is embellished with more strips of hide. The cattle of each regiment or *iButho* were of the same colour as their hide shields to create a uniform appearance. White shields belonged to the oldest regiment, while the youngest regiment's shields were black. Weapons and shields, like everything else in traditional society, were made by specially-appointed members of the community, and blacksmiths and leather makers were and still are regarded as specialists in their craft.

• ZULU TRIBAL HERITAGE •

OF WIVES AND WOMEN

In traditional Zulu society women are regarded as secondary in status to men. A woman defers not only to her husband, but to his male relatives, particularly to his father and his brothers. A man, likewise, is honoured not only by his wives, but by his daughters and daughters-in-law. A woman has no right of ownership; whatever property (such as cattle) she brings with her when marrying, becomes her husband's. If he dies, ownership usually reverts to a senior male relative. Polygamous marriages are still common today. To take a wife, a man pays a dowry in the form of cattle, known as *lobolo*. He may take as many wives as he can afford, and his wives often dress in a uniform style. In every household there is a senior wife, and

• ROLE OF WOMEN •

each of the wives has her own place and knows what her privileges and obligations are. A junior wife has to be careful not to outshine her elders. Sharing her man as she does with other wives, a woman's closest bonds are with her children. The physical demands of life are great. In addition to her household duties, agriculture is also her responsibility. Women are expected to work the land and cultivate crops such as maize, sorghum, groundnuts and beans. They regularly carry heavy loads of fire wood, provisions or containers of water on their heads, often over great distances.

• ZULU TRIBAL HERITAGE •

SKINS, PELTS AND PLUMES

Styles of traditional dress vary from clan to clan, and from one area to another. Zulus dress according to their different age groups, and clothing is directly related to the status of the wearer. Everyday clothing tends to be simple. Men wear a leather belt with strips of hide hanging down the front and rear, while young girls often wear the same, or a simple skirt wrapped around the body. Married women wear heavy, pleated skirts of ox-hide which are usually made for them by their husbands. Their large, structured headdresses are constructed from course knitting wool, sometimes woven into their own hair, and bound together with clay. These headdresses vary from region to region, and are always an indication of their wearers' married status, as short hair is favoured by unmarried women. Pregnant women can often be seen wearing a maternity apron of antelope skin which is said to make the expected child swift, agile and full of grace. Ceremonial dress is elaborate,

• TRADITIONAL DRESS •

with magnificent displays of beadwork offsetting the finery of skins, pelts, plumes and feathers. Choice of skins is often restricted according to status: traditionally the leopard skin may only be worn by members of royalty, principally chiefs and most notably, the king. Any leopard killed becomes the chief's property. A ceremonial shield is frequently seen as part of a man's regalia when he goes out. Zulu warriors wore special clothing to denote their regiments, sometimes covering their bodies in cowhides, or wearing embellishments such as an otter skin headband or a colourful array of feathers.

11

• ZULU TRIBAL HERITAGE •

CEREMONIES AND CELEBRATIONS

Ceremonies play a major role in Zulu life as they do in all traditional societies. Dance, music and beer-drinking accompany occasions as diverse as the coming of age of a girl or boy; marriage; and funerals *(opposite left)* among others, as well as regimental traditions such as the 'washing of the spears' and the 'wiping of the axe'. Although ancestor worship is the traditional Zulu religion, Christian sects such as the Shembi cult *(above right)* are also

• RITUALS AND CUSTOMS •

prevalent in many rural areas. Drums made of tightly-stretched oxhide *(above)* play a major role in ceremonial music-making and dancing. These need the constant attention of their owners as they tend to slacken in the humid conditions of KwaZulu-Natal and need to be re-tightened. Many ceremonies are protracted, hospitable affairs, sometimes stretching over three days or more. They usually last as long as there is food and drink for the guests and family members to enjoy. During the three-day bridal ceremony, a bride *(opposite left and below)* spends much of her time sitting quietly in a special hut with her bridesmaids. The fringe over her eyes is part of the practice of respect, or *hlonipha*, which is accorded to her suitor and his father.

• ZULU TRIBAL HERITAGE •

SANGOMAS

The Zulus believe their daily lives are guided by the spirits of their ancestors, or *Amadlozi,* and make sacrifices to them to ensure that they look favourably upon them. Ancestors are only seen in dreams, and a diviner or *sangoma* alone has special powers to communicate with them. People consult a *sangoma* if a simple sacrifice has failed to bring about the desired result. Diviners are called to their profession by their ancestors, and at first are apprenticed to a teacher and trained to contact the ancestral spirits as a source of inspiration. This enables them to diagnose misfortune and illness. They also locate lost or stolen objects and tell fortunes through the medium of bone-throwing *(left)*. In this profession women outnumber the men, who have

• DIVINERS AND HEALERS •

adopted the distinctive beaded attire of their female counterparts - the long wigs threaded with white beads and the crossed breast bands of animal skin. Topping their headdresses are inflated bladders of animals which have been sacrificed to ancestors in order to augment the wearers' power of 'sight' into the spiritual world. This regalia sets diviners apart from ordinary members of society and proclaims their supernatural powers. The belief that they alone are able to mediate between people and their ancestral spirits gives them considerable influence. The beads on a *sangoma's* head-dress are said to be strung in loops so that the spirits they call up have somewhere to sit as they speak into their ears. A *sangoma* often works in conjunction with a herbalist or traditional medicinal healer known as an *iNyanga (opposite above)*.

• ZULU TRIBAL HERITAGE •

COURTSHIP AND BETROTHAL

Courtship among the rural Zulu is subject to strict observance of protocol. During adolescence girls become members of a number of successive 'guilds' or peer groups until they reach the stage where they are of a marriageable age. A young man who wishes to woo a girl may only do so if she is considered to be suitably mature and has come of age - and only if her peers *(above right)* consider he will make her a good husband. The suitor then has to prepare the way ahead carefully through a series of indirect approaches which are sometimes undertaken by his sisters acting on his behalf. After a period during which

• COURTSHIP •

she is expected to play 'hard to get', the girl indicates her acceptance of the young man's attentions by giving him a gift of betrothal beads *(above)*. Once the girl's family have indicated their approval of the engagement, the young man flies a white flag outside his homestead to show that he will soon be taking a bride. In the interests of diplomacy, the *lobolo* or 'bride price' negotiations which follow between the young man and the bride's father are usually conducted by close family members of both parties rather than by the principal players themselves. As each clan is regarded as one large family there is a strict law among the Zulu that members of the same clan may not marry – no matter how far back the original family link may go and even if it can no longer be traced.

• ZULU TRIBAL HERITAGE •

GROWING UP

From early childhood Zulus learn to respect their elders and to regard their peers as equals. As they grow up they associate formally with groupings of other children of their own age and sex. Young boys herd cattle and goats while their elder brothers assist with milking cows. Girls clean the huts, collect water and firewood, and help in the fields. These pastimes ensure that young Zulus grow up physically independent and strong. As schooling did not exist in the old days, children learnt their

• EARLY YEARS •

history and customs through the idiom of story-telling. To this day, the oral tradition of the Zulu still prevails, especially in rural communities. The example of elders also played an important role in education and boys would play games which helped to teach them the skills of warfare and fighting. As traditional Zulu family units have always been large, children, especially girls, assist in carrying and tending to their younger brothers and sisters. It is common to see a child of five or six 'piggy-backing' a small infant which is tied to its back with a blanket. At the age of ten or eleven, girls also share in the duties of cooking. In their mid-teens, they were often considered to have reached a marriageable age, although these days this has tended to shift until later in life.

• ZULU TRIBAL HERITAGE •

A PLACE OF SHELTER

Traditional Zulu beehive huts are made exclusively from natural materials. They comprise a framework of saplings covered with plaited grass or rushes harvested from the riverside. While techniques of hut-making vary from clan to clan, construction of the huts is usually carried out by men. The saplings are bent and bound to form the classic beehive shape, before being covered with thatching grass. Women reap the thatching grass and weave the grass roping which is used to bind it. Thatching, a skill for which the Zulus are justly famous, is an activity which both men and women ably perform, depending on the region. Besides the traditional beehive huts, many Zulu abodes these days are constructed from wattle and daub with thatch (or galvanized iron) roofing.

• HOMES AND HERDS •

SYMBOLS OF WEALTH

Whether milking, or ploughing with a team of oxen, the tending of cattle is regarded as a male activity. A Zulu's cattle are his pride and joy. They are both the symbols of a man's wealth, and the currency by which it is measured. Only men generally enter the cattle kraal which is regarded as sacred and is invariably found in every Zulu *uMuzi*, from the simplest homestead to the home of the king himself. A Zulu knows the individual characteristics of each of his animals, and can identify a beast at a moment's notice, even in a large herd.

• ZULU TRIBAL HERITAGE •

HEARTH AND HOME

Zulu society is underpinned by close-knit family units. Men, women and children come together from their separate chores to spend their leisure time sharing a meal, whether indoors or around a fire outside. The daily diet of the Zulu is usually a simple one of maize, sorghum, sweet potatoes, melons and pumpkin, eaten with curdled milk known as *amasi*. Food is simply prepared, the maize roasted on the cob, or ground and boiled to form a stiff, lumpy porridge known as *phuthu*. Cast iron pots are widely used in rural Zulu homesteads these days. Elaborate meals with meat are usually reserved for special occasions, or for ceremonies such as

• MAIZE AND MALT •

the harvest festival which is traditionally held in December or January when the crops are ripe. Zulu beer or *umQombothi*, made of sorghum, is always popular. This is prepared by women who strain the fermented liquid through long cylinder-shaped sieves, woven from grass, to separate the husks before it is drunk. Good manners are particularly important during meal times. Food is savoured over leisurely conversation, and is generally eaten by hand. People sit on grass mats during indoor meals, the men on the right hand side of the hut, the women opposite them. Music making is seldom absent from Zulu life *(right)*, and is as integral a part of daily routine as it is during the various ceremonial events that punctuate the year.

• ZULU TRIBAL HERITAGE •

SAY IT WITH BEADS

The art of Zulu beadwork has evolved from a tradition cultivated over countless generations. This dates back centuries to the time of the early white traders who first introduced colourful glass beads as a bartering medium. Zulu beadwork encompasses a symbolic language which may indicate coded love messages, a wearer's age or status, his or her home area - and demonstrates a superb use of colour and innovative design. Besides its function as jewellery, Zulu beadwork is commonly found decorating aprons, as beaded panels, on headdresses and embellishing the heads of ceremonial sticks.

ZULU BEADWORK

• ZULU TRIBAL HERITAGE •

ARTEFACTS AND ORNAMENTS

Besides their beadwork, the Zulus' artistic leanings are widely expressed in a diversity of crafts which are employed both to make and to decorate items used in daily life. Traditionally, woodcarving is a male skill which is taught from childhood. Boys and men are adept at using small iron knives and choppers to make bowls, platters, combs, spoons, ceremonial sticks, spear handles and headrests to protect their elaborate headdresses. Other items include ornaments such as animal carvings or masks. Zulu women are

• HANDICRAFTS •

known for their expertise as grass weavers and make a wide variety of elaborate basketware and mats *(above)*. The choice of grass used denotes the purpose for which an item is intended. For instance, a mat woven out of fine, highly-prized *ncema* grass is used for a bridal mat, as opposed to a more common, course grass, which would serve a more mundane function. Zulus are also renowned as potters, generally using the coil method by rolling the clay into long thin strips and winding these around to fashion their pots. A sharp stone is used to smooth surfaces, which are also often embellished with intricate patterns. The pots are dried in the sun, then fired by burying them in hot ashes around a fire.

• ZULU TRIBAL HERITAGE •

CULTURAL SHOWCASE

Ethnic culture has always been a great draw card among foreign tourists who visit this country. The ever-potent fascination for the Zulu has proved one of the mainstays of the tourism industry in KwaZulu-Natal over the years. One of the most popular resorts in this regard is Shakaland, near Eshowe. Adapted from and built on the set of the television series *Shaka Zulu*, this is run as an hotel and offers an excellent interpretive programme of classical Shakan Zulu culture which is still practised during Zulu ceremonies today. The programme features dancing, stick fighting, a wide variety of social

• TRADITIONAL VILLAGES •

customs of traditional life in an authentic Zulu village. Specific attention is drawn to the roles and social functions of diviners, blacksmiths and medicinal healers. These interesting aspects of Zulu culture can also be experienced at Dumazulu village near Hluhluwe. Simunye, a lodge near Melmoth which is modelled on an early pioneer settlement, focuses on the inter-relations of black and white people since the Anglo-Zulu wars, and on the ever-changing lifestyle of the rural Zulu today. A trip to Mkuzi Game Reserve in Maputaland should include a visit to the KwaJobe cultural village situated within its borders. This will provide an interesting insight into the lifestyle of a northern Zulu clan.

• ZULU TRIBAL HERITAGE •

RURAL DEVELOPMENT

As the 20th century draws to a close, many remote parts of KwaZulu-Natal *(right)* are populated by Zulu people whose lifestyle is still solidly based on the time-honoured traditions of their ancestors *(above)*. Here, a person's world is still an intensely local one, the focus never far from the home and its immediate environment, and 'civilisation' seldom extends closer than the nearest trading store. But even in these parts, modern developments have begun to encroach as migrant workers *(opposite right)* return home from the cities with new-fangled goods such as a portable

• TRANSITION •

radio, a highly polished item of furniture, or a bicycle. These incongruous items can be seen jostling for attention in a yard or a hut alongside traditional Zulu articles. Modern education facilities are opening up, and, increasingly, tourism is playing a constructive role in boosting the economies of rural Zulu communities. These have begun to reap the benefits of extended markets for selling crafts or for finding employment. Members of rural communities are finding opportunities for self-development through the infrastructure of power lines and roads which lead to game parks in remote, otherwise inaccessible, areas. This has made possible the building of new classrooms, the introduction of electricity, the availability of water, and small business development along the lines of small informal shops, market gardens, roadside craft markets *(above left)* and home produce stalls.

• ZULU TRIBAL HERITAGE •

STRENGTH OF TRADITION

The characteristics of physical strength and courage, coupled with an indelible sense of their own history, has ensured that the Zulu have maintained a national identity despite developments which have occurred around them over the past 200 years. However, they have always had a free-wheeling attitude towards cultural borrowing, both from people who have been absorbed into the mainstream of Zulu culture itself, and from outside influences such as the white man. This is manifested both in physical terms (such as in adopted styles of dress, for instance) and in new-found language idioms. This healthy flexibility, combined with their steadfast sense of pride in who they are and what they represent, has ensured that the Zulu people have remained a vibrant force in South African society today.